THIS JOURNAL

Belongs to....

My Trips!

Location	When/How Long?
1)_____	
2)_____	
3)_____	
4)_____	
5)_____	
6)_____	

Extra Notes

_____

_____

_____

_____

_____

_____

My Trips!

Location	When/How Long?
7)_____	
8)_____	
9)_____	
10)_____	
11)_____	
12)_____	

Extra Notes

_____
_____
_____
_____
_____

Where Am I? _____

Date: _____
M T W T F S S

WEATHER REPORT:

Hot   Mild
Cloudy   Stormy
Raining   windy
Snowing   Sunny
cold   Hail
OTHER?: _____

TODAY I FEEL...

Circle one!

BEST THING ABOUT TODAY?

_____
_____
_____
_____
_____

WHAT I DID TODAY..........DRAW, DOODLE, STICK!

3 things i learnt!

1)_____ ☐

2)_____ ☐

3)_____ ☐

One interesting fact about today?

_____
_____
_____
_____

Your FREE Space! Go craazzy!

Where Am I? _____

WEATHER REPORT:

Hot	Mild
Cloudy	Stormy
Raining	windy
Snowing	Sunny
cold	Hail

OTHER?: _____

TODAY I FEEL...

Circle one!

BEST THING ABOUT TODAY?

_____
_____
_____
_____
_____

WHAT I DID TODAY...........DRAW, DOODLE, STICK!

3 things i learnt!

1)_____ ☐

2)_____ ☐

3)_____ ☐

One interesting fact about today?

_____
_____
_____
_____

Did you try anything new today?

Where Am I? _____

Date: [_____]
M T W T F S S

WEATHER REPORT:

Hot	Mild
Cloudy	Stormy
Raining	windy
Snowing	Sunny
cold	Hail

OTHER?: _____

TODAY I FEEL...

Circle one!

BEST THING ABOUT TODAY?

_____
_____
_____
_____
_____

WHAT I DID TODAY..........DRAW, DOODLE, STICK!

3 things i learnt!

1)_____ ☐

2)_____ ☐

3)_____ ☐

One interesting fact about today?

_____
_____
_____
_____

Did you eat anything delicious today?

Where Am I?_____

Date:
M T W T F S S

WEATHER REPORT:

Hot   Mild
Cloudy   Stormy
Raining   windy
Snowing   Sunny
cold   Hail
OTHER?: _____

TODAY I FEEL...

Circle one!

BEST THING ABOUT TODAY?

WHAT I DID TODAY..........DRAW, DOODLE, STICK!

3 things i learnt!
1)_____ ☐
2)_____ ☐
3)_____ ☐

One interesting fact about today?

Anything you can stick in? e.g. tickets!

Where Am I? _____

WEATHER REPORT:

Hot	Mild
Cloudy	Stormy
Raining	windy
Snowing	Sunny
cold	Hail

OTHER?: _____

TODAY I FEEL...

Circle one!

BEST THING ABOUT TODAY?

_____
_____
_____
_____
_____

WHAT I DID TODAY..........DRAW, DOODLE, STICK!

3 things i learnt!

1)_____ ☐

2)_____ ☐

3)_____ ☐

One interesting fact about today?

_____
_____
_____
_____
_____

Did You See anything strange or unusual today?

Where Am I? _____

WEATHER REPORT:

Hot	Mild
Cloudy	Stormy
Raining	windy
Snowing	Sunny
cold	Hail

OTHER?: _____

TODAY I FEEL...

Circle one!

BEST THING ABOUT TODAY?

_____
_____
_____
_____
_____

WHAT I DID TODAY..........DRAW, DOODLE, STICK!

3 things i learnt!

1)_____ ☐

2)_____ ☐

3)_____ ☐

One interesting fact about today?

_____
_____
_____
_____

Visit any new places today?

Where Am I? _____

Date: _____
M T W T F S S

WEATHER REPORT:

Hot	Mild
Cloudy	Stormy
Raining	windy
Snowing	Sunny
cold	Hail

OTHER?: _____

TODAY I FEEL...

Circle one!

BEST THING ABOUT TODAY?

_____
_____
_____
_____
_____

WHAT I DID TODAY..........DRAW, DOODLE, STICK!

3 things i learnt!

1) _____ ☐

2) _____ ☐

3) _____ ☐

One interesting fact about today?

_____
_____
_____
_____

Pick a great memory - doodle about it?

Where Am I?_____

Date: _____

M T W T F S S

WEATHER REPORT:

Hot   Mild

Cloudy   Stormy

Raining   windy

Snowing Sunny

cold   Hail

OTHER?: _____

TODAY I FEEL...

Circle one!

BEST THING ABOUT TODAY?

WHAT I DID TODAY..........DRAW, DOODLE, STICK!

3 things i learnt!

1)_____ ☐

2)_____ ☐

3)_____ ☐

One interesting fact about today?

Your FREE Space! Go craazzy!

Where Am I? _____

WEATHER REPORT:

Hot	Mild
Cloudy	Stormy
Raining	windy
Snowing	Sunny
cold	Hail

OTHER?: _____

TODAY I FEEL...

Circle one!

BEST THING ABOUT TODAY?

_____
_____
_____
_____
_____

WHAT I DID TODAY..........DRAW, DOODLE, STICK!

3 things i learnt!

1)_____ ☐

2)_____ ☐

3)_____ ☐

One interesting fact about today?

_____
_____
_____
_____
_____

Did you try anything new today?

Where Am I?_____

WEATHER REPORT:

Hot   Mild

Cloudy   Stormy

Raining   windy

Snowing Sunny

cold   Hail

OTHER?: _____

TODAY I FEEL...

Circle one!

BEST THING ABOUT TODAY?

_____
_____
_____
_____
_____

WHAT I DID TODAY..........DRAW, DOODLE, STICK!

3 things i learnt!

1)_____ ☐

2)_____ ☐

3)_____ ☐

One interesting fact about today?
_____
_____
_____
_____
_____

Did you eat anything delicious today?

_____
_____
_____
_____
_____
_____
_____
_____
_____
_____
_____
_____
_____
_____
_____
_____
_____
_____

Where Am I? _____

Date: _____

M T W T F S S

WEATHER REPORT:

Hot   Mild

Cloudy   Stormy

Raining   windy

Snowing   Sunny

cold   Hail

OTHER?: _____

TODAY I FEEL...

Circle one!

BEST THING ABOUT TODAY?

_____
_____
_____
_____
_____
_____

WHAT I DID TODAY..........DRAW, DOODLE, STICK!

3 things i learnt!

1)_____ ☐

2)_____ ☐

3)_____ ☐

One interesting fact about today?

_____
_____
_____
_____

Anything you can stick in? e.g. tickets!

Where Am I? _____

Date: [   ]
M T W T F S S

WEATHER REPORT:

Hot	Mild
Cloudy	Stormy
Raining	windy
Snowing	Sunny
cold	Hail

OTHER?: _____

TODAY I FEEL...

Circle one!

BEST THING ABOUT TODAY?

_____
_____
_____
_____
_____

WHAT I DID TODAY..........DRAW, DOODLE, STICK!

3 things i learnt!

1)_____ ☐

2)_____ ☐

3)_____ ☐

One interesting fact about today?
_____
_____
_____
_____

Did you see anything strange or unusual today?

Where Am I?_____

Date: _____
M T W T F S S

WEATHER REPORT:

Hot   Mild
Cloudy   Stormy
Raining   windy
Snowing   Sunny
cold   Hail
OTHER?: _____

TODAY I FEEL...

Circle one!

BEST THING ABOUT TODAY?

_____
_____
_____
_____
_____

WHAT I DID TODAY..........DRAW, DOODLE, STICK!

3 things i learnt!
1)_____ ☐
2)_____ ☐
3)_____ ☐

One interesting fact about today?
_____
_____
_____
_____
_____

Visit any new places today?

Where Am I?_____

WEATHER REPORT:

Hot	Mild
Cloudy	Stormy
Raining	windy
Snowing	Sunny
cold	Hail

OTHER?: _____

TODAY I FEEL...

Circle one!

BEST THING ABOUT TODAY?

WHAT I DID TODAY..........DRAW, DOODLE, STICK!

3 things i learnt!

1)_____ ☐

2)_____ ☐

3)_____ ☐

One interesting fact about today?

Pick a great memory - doodle about it?

Where Am I?_____

WEATHER REPORT:

Hot	Mild
Cloudy	Stormy
Raining	windy
Snowing	Sunny
cold	Hail

OTHER?: _____

TODAY I FEEL...

Circle one!

BEST THING ABOUT TODAY?

_____
_____
_____
_____
_____

WHAT I DID TODAY..........DRAW, DOODLE, STICK!

3 things i learnt!

1)_____ ☐

2)_____ ☐

3)_____ ☐

One interesting fact about today?

_____
_____
_____
_____
_____

Your FREE Space! Go craazzy!

Where Am I? _____

WEATHER REPORT:

Hot	Mild
Cloudy	Stormy
Raining	windy
Snowing	Sunny
cold	Hail

OTHER?: _____

TODAY I FEEL...

Circle one!

BEST THING ABOUT TODAY?

_____
_____
_____
_____
_____
_____

WHAT I DID TODAY..........DRAW, DOODLE, STICK!

3 things i learnt!

1) _____ ☐

2) _____ ☐

3) _____ ☐

One interesting fact about today?

_____
_____
_____
_____

Did you try anything new today?

Where Am I? _____

Date: [ ]

M T W T F S S

WEATHER REPORT:

Hot	Mild
Cloudy	Stormy
Raining	windy
Snowing	Sunny
cold	Hail

OTHER?: _____

TODAY I FEEL...

Circle one!

BEST THING ABOUT TODAY?

_____
_____
_____
_____
_____
_____

WHAT I DID TODAY..........DRAW, DOODLE, STICK!

3 things i learnt!

1)_____ ☐

2)_____ ☐

3)_____ ☐

One interesting fact about today?

_____
_____
_____
_____

Did you eat anything delicious today?

Where Am I? _____

WEATHER REPORT:

Hot	Mild
Cloudy	Stormy
Raining	windy
Snowing	Sunny
cold	Hail

OTHER?: _____

TODAY I FEEL...

Circle one!

BEST THING ABOUT TODAY?

_____
_____
_____
_____
_____

WHAT I DID TODAY..........DRAW, DOODLE, STICK!

3 things i learnt!

1)_____ ☐

2)_____ ☐

3)_____ ☐

One interesting fact about today?

_____
_____
_____
_____

Anything you can stick in? e.g. tickets!

Where Am I? _____

Date:
M T W T F S S

WEATHER REPORT:

Hot	Mild
Cloudy	Stormy
Raining	windy
Snowing	Sunny
cold	Hail

OTHER?: _____

TODAY I FEEL...

Circle one!

BEST THING ABOUT TODAY?

_____
_____
_____
_____
_____

WHAT I DID TODAY...........DRAW, DOODLE, STICK!

3 things i learnt!
1)_____ ☐
2)_____ ☐
3)_____ ☐

One interesting fact about today?
_____
_____
_____
_____
_____

Did You See anything strange or unusual today?

Where Am I? _____

Date: [box]
M T W T F S S

WEATHER REPORT:

Hot   Mild

Cloudy   Stormy

Raining   windy

Snowing   Sunny

cold   Hail

OTHER?: _____

TODAY I FEEL...

Circle one!

BEST THING ABOUT TODAY?

_____
_____
_____
_____
_____

WHAT I DID TODAY..........DRAW, DOODLE, STICK!

---

3 things i learnt!

1)_____ ☐

2)_____ ☐

3)_____ ☐

One interesting fact about today?

_____
_____
_____
_____
_____

Visit any new places today?

Where Am I? _____

WEATHER REPORT:

Hot	Mild
Cloudy	Stormy
Raining	windy
Snowing	Sunny
cold	Hail

OTHER?: _____

TODAY I FEEL...

Circle one!

BEST THING ABOUT TODAY?

_____
_____
_____
_____
_____

WHAT I DID TODAY..........DRAW, DOODLE, STICK!

3 things i learnt!

1) _____ ☐

2) _____ ☐

3) _____ ☐

One interesting fact about today?

_____
_____
_____
_____
_____

Pick a great memory - doodle about it?

_____
_____
_____
_____
_____
_____
_____
_____
_____
_____
_____
_____
_____
_____
_____
_____
_____
_____

Where Am I?_____

WEATHER REPORT:

Hot	Mild
Cloudy	Stormy
Raining	windy
Snowing	Sunny
cold	Hail

OTHER?: _____

TODAY I FEEL...

Circle one!

BEST THING ABOUT TODAY?

_____
_____
_____
_____
_____
_____

WHAT I DID TODAY..........DRAW, DOODLE, STICK!

3 things i learnt!

1)_____ ☐

2)_____ ☐

3)_____ ☐

One interesting fact about today?

_____
_____
_____
_____
_____

Your FREE space! Go craazzy!

Where Am I? _____

WEATHER REPORT:

Hot	Mild
Cloudy	Stormy
Raining	windy
Snowing	Sunny
cold	Hail

OTHER?: _____

TODAY I FEEL...

Circle one!

BEST THING ABOUT TODAY?

_____
_____
_____
_____
_____
_____

WHAT I DID TODAY..........DRAW, DOODLE, STICK!

3 things i learnt!
1)_____ ☐
2)_____ ☐
3)_____ ☐

One interesting fact about today?
_____
_____
_____
_____

Did you try anything new today?

_____
_____
_____
_____
_____
_____
_____
_____
_____
_____
_____
_____
_____
_____
_____

Where Am I? _____

Date: _____
M T W T F S S

WEATHER REPORT:

Hot	Mild
Cloudy	Stormy
Raining	windy
Snowing	Sunny
cold	Hail

OTHER?: _____

TODAY I FEEL...

Circle one!

BEST THING ABOUT TODAY?

_____
_____
_____
_____
_____

WHAT I DID TODAY.........DRAW, DOODLE, STICK!

3 things i learnt!

1)_____ ☐

2)_____ ☐

3)_____ ☐

One interesting fact about today?

_____
_____
_____
_____
_____

Did you eat anything delicious today?

Where Am I?_____

Date: _____
M T W T F S S

WEATHER REPORT:

Hot   Mild
Cloudy   Stormy
Raining   windy
Snowing   Sunny
cold   Hail
OTHER?: _____

TODAY I FEEL...

Circle one!

BEST THING ABOUT TODAY?

_____
_____
_____
_____
_____
_____

WHAT I DID TODAY..........DRAW, DOODLE, STICK!

3 things i learnt!

1)_____ ☐
2)_____ ☐
3)_____ ☐

One interesting fact about today?

_____
_____
_____
_____

Anything you can stick in? e.g. tickets!

Where Am I?_____

WEATHER REPORT:

Hot	Mild
Cloudy	Stormy
Raining	windy
Snowing	Sunny
cold	Hail

OTHER?: _____

TODAY I FEEL...

Circle one!

BEST THING ABOUT TODAY?

_____

_____

_____

_____

_____

WHAT I DID TODAY..........DRAW, DOODLE, STICK!

3 things i learnt!

1)_____ ☐

2)_____ ☐

3)_____ ☐

One interesting fact about today?

_____

_____

_____

_____

Did You See anything strange or unusual today?

Where Am I? _____

Date: _____
M T W T F S S

WEATHER REPORT:

Hot   Mild
Cloudy   Stormy
Raining   windy
Snowing   Sunny
cold   Hail
OTHER?: _____

TODAY I FEEL...

Circle one!

BEST THING ABOUT TODAY?

_____
_____
_____
_____
_____

WHAT I DID TODAY..........DRAW, DOODLE, STICK!

3 things i learnt!
1)_____ ☐
2)_____ ☐
3)_____ ☐

One interesting fact about today?
_____
_____
_____
_____

Visit any new places today?

_____
_____
_____
_____
_____
_____
_____
_____
_____
_____
_____
_____
_____
_____

Where Am I? _____

WEATHER REPORT:

Hot   Mild
Cloudy   Stormy
Raining   windy
Snowing   Sunny
cold   Hail
OTHER?: _____

TODAY I FEEL...

Circle one!

BEST THING ABOUT TODAY?

_____
_____
_____
_____
_____

WHAT I DID TODAY..........DRAW, DOODLE, STICK!

3 things i learnt!

1) _____ ☐

2) _____ ☐

3) _____ ☐

One interesting fact about today?
_____
_____
_____
_____

Pick a great memory - doodle about it?

Where Am I? _____

WEATHER REPORT:

Hot	Mild
Cloudy	Stormy
Raining	windy
Snowing	Sunny
cold	Hail

OTHER?: _____

TODAY I FEEL...

Circle one!

BEST THING ABOUT TODAY?

_____
_____
_____
_____
_____

WHAT I DID TODAY..........DRAW, DOODLE, STICK!

3 things i learnt!

1)_____ ☐

2)_____ ☐

3)_____ ☐

One interesting fact about today?
_____
_____
_____
_____

Your FREE Space! Go craazzy!

Where Am I?_____

WEATHER REPORT:

Hot   Mild
Cloudy   Stormy
Raining   windy
Snowing   Sunny
cold   Hail
OTHER?: _____

TODAY I FEEL...

Circle one!

BEST THING ABOUT TODAY?

WHAT I DID TODAY..........DRAW, DOODLE, STICK!

3 things i learnt!
1)_____ ☐
2)_____ ☐
3)_____ ☐

One interesting fact about today?

Did you try anything new today?

Where Am I? _____

Date: _____
M T W T F S S

WEATHER REPORT:

Hot	Mild
Cloudy	Stormy
Raining	windy
Snowing	Sunny
cold	Hail

OTHER?: _____

TODAY I FEEL...

Circle one!

BEST THING ABOUT TODAY?

_____
_____
_____
_____
_____

WHAT I DID TODAY..........DRAW, DOODLE, STICK!

3 things i learnt!

1)_____ ☐

2)_____ ☐

3)_____ ☐

One interesting fact about today?

_____
_____
_____
_____

Did you eat anything delicious today?

Where Am I? _____

WEATHER REPORT:

Hot	Mild
Cloudy	Stormy
Raining	windy
Snowing	Sunny
cold	Hail

OTHER?: _____

TODAY I FEEL...

Circle one!

BEST THING ABOUT TODAY?

_____
_____
_____
_____
_____

WHAT I DID TODAY..........DRAW, DOODLE, STICK!

3 things i learnt!

1) _____ ☐

2) _____ ☐

3) _____ ☐

One interesting fact about today?

_____
_____
_____
_____
_____

Anything you can stick in? e.g. tickets!

Where Am I? _____

Date: [_____]
M T W T F S S

WEATHER REPORT:

Hot	Mild
Cloudy	Stormy
Raining	windy
Snowing	Sunny
cold	Hail

OTHER?: _____

TODAY I FEEL...

Circle one!

BEST THING ABOUT TODAY?

_____
_____
_____
_____
_____

WHAT I DID TODAY..........DRAW, DOODLE, STICK!

3 things i learnt!

1)_____ ☐

2)_____ ☐

3)_____ ☐

One interesting fact about today?

_____
_____
_____
_____
_____

Did You See anything strange or unusual today?

Where Am I? _____

Date: _____

M T W T F S S

WEATHER REPORT:

Hot   Mild

Cloudy   Stormy

Raining   windy

Snowing   Sunny

cold   Hail

OTHER?: _____

TODAY I FEEL...

Circle one!

BEST THING ABOUT TODAY?

_____
_____
_____
_____
_____
_____

WHAT I DID TODAY..........DRAW, DOODLE, STICK!

3 things i learnt!

1) _____ ☐

2) _____ ☐

3) _____ ☐

One interesting fact about today?

_____
_____
_____
_____

Visit any new places today?

Where Am I? _____

WEATHER REPORT:

Hot   Mild
Cloudy   Stormy
Raining   windy
Snowing   Sunny
cold   Hail
OTHER?: _____

TODAY I FEEL...

Circle one!

BEST THING ABOUT TODAY?

_____
_____
_____
_____
_____
_____

WHAT I DID TODAY..........DRAW, DOODLE, STICK!

3 things i learnt!

1)_____ ☐

2)_____ ☐

3)_____ ☐

One interesting fact about today?
_____
_____
_____
_____

Pick a great memory - doodle about it?

_____
_____
_____
_____
_____
_____
_____
_____
_____
_____
_____
_____
_____
_____
_____
_____
_____

Where Am I? _____

Date: [ ]

M T W T F S S

WEATHER REPORT:

Hot	Mild
Cloudy	Stormy
Raining	windy
Snowing	Sunny
cold	Hail

OTHER?: _____

TODAY I FEEL...

Circle one!

BEST THING ABOUT TODAY?

_____
_____
_____
_____
_____

WHAT I DID TODAY..........DRAW, DOODLE, STICK!

3 things i learnt!

1)_____ ☐

2)_____ ☐

3)_____ ☐

One interesting fact about today?

_____
_____
_____
_____
_____

Your FREE Space! Go craazzy!

Where Am I?_____

Date: [_____]
M T W T F S S

WEATHER REPORT:

Hot   Mild
Cloudy   Stormy
Raining   windy
Snowing   Sunny
cold   Hail
OTHER?: _____

TODAY I FEEL...

Circle one!

BEST THING ABOUT TODAY?

WHAT I DID TODAY..........DRAW, DOODLE, STICK!

3 things i learnt!

1)_____ ☐

2)_____ ☐

3)_____ ☐

One interesting fact about today?

Did you try anything new today?

Where Am I?_____

WEATHER REPORT:

Hot	Mild
Cloudy	Stormy
Raining	windy
Snowing	Sunny
cold	Hail

OTHER?: _____

TODAY I FEEL...

Circle one!

BEST THING ABOUT TODAY?

WHAT I DID TODAY..........DRAW, DOODLE, STICK!

3 things i learnt!

1)_____ ☐

2)_____ ☐

3)_____ ☐

One interesting fact about today?

Did you eat anything delicious today?

Where Am I? _____

WEATHER REPORT:

Hot   Mild

Cloudy   Stormy

Raining   windy

Snowing   Sunny

cold   Hail

OTHER?: _____

TODAY I FEEL...

Circle one!

BEST THING ABOUT TODAY?

WHAT I DID TODAY..........DRAW, DOODLE, STICK!

3 things i learnt!

1)_____ ☐

2)_____ ☐

3)_____ ☐

One interesting fact about today?

Anything you can stick in? e.g. tickets!

Where Am I? _____

Date: _____
M T W T F S S

WEATHER REPORT:

Hot   Mild
Cloudy   Stormy
Raining   windy
Snowing   Sunny
cold   Hail
OTHER?: _____

TODAY I FEEL...

Circle one!

BEST THING ABOUT TODAY?

_____
_____
_____
_____
_____
_____

WHAT I DID TODAY..........DRAW, DOODLE, STICK!

3 things i learnt!

1)_____ ☐
2)_____ ☐
3)_____ ☐

One interesting fact about today?

_____
_____
_____
_____

Did you see anything strange or unusual today?

Where Am I? _____

WEATHER REPORT:

Hot	Mild
Cloudy	Stormy
Raining	windy
Snowing	Sunny
cold	Hail

OTHER?: _____

TODAY I FEEL...

Circle one!

BEST THING ABOUT TODAY?

_____
_____
_____
_____
_____

WHAT I DID TODAY..........DRAW, DOODLE, STICK!

3 things i learnt!

1)_____ ☐

2)_____ ☐

3)_____ ☐

One interesting fact about today?
_____
_____
_____
_____

Visit any new places today?

Where Am I? _____

WEATHER REPORT:

Hot	Mild
Cloudy	Stormy
Raining	windy
Snowing	Sunny
cold	Hail

OTHER?: _____

TODAY I FEEL...

Circle one!

BEST THING ABOUT TODAY?

_____
_____
_____
_____
_____

WHAT I DID TODAY..........DRAW, DOODLE, STICK!

3 things i learnt!

1)_____ ☐

2)_____ ☐

3)_____ ☐

One interesting fact about today?

_____
_____
_____
_____
_____

Pick a great memory - doodle about it?

Where Am I? _____

Date: _____

M T W T F S S

WEATHER REPORT:

Hot   Mild

Cloudy   Stormy

Raining   windy

Snowing   Sunny

cold   Hail

OTHER?: _____

TODAY I FEEL...

Circle one!

BEST THING ABOUT TODAY?

_____
_____
_____
_____
_____

WHAT I DID TODAY.........DRAW, DOODLE, STICK!

3 things i learnt!

1)_____ ☐

2)_____ ☐

3)_____ ☐

One interesting fact about today?

_____
_____
_____
_____

Your FREE Space! Go craazzy!

Where Am I?_____

Date: _____
M T W T F S S

WEATHER REPORT:

Hot   Mild
Cloudy   Stormy
Raining   windy
Snowing   Sunny
cold   Hail
OTHER?: _____

TODAY I FEEL...

Circle one!

BEST THING ABOUT TODAY?

WHAT I DID TODAY...........DRAW, DOODLE, STICK!

3 things i learnt!

1) _____ ☐

2) _____ ☐

3) _____ ☐

One interesting fact about today?

Did you try anything new today?

Where Am I?_____

WEATHER REPORT:

Hot	Mild
Cloudy	Stormy
Raining	windy
Snowing	Sunny
cold	Hail

OTHER?: _____

TODAY I FEEL...

Circle one!

BEST THING ABOUT TODAY?

_____
_____
_____
_____
_____

WHAT I DID TODAY..........DRAW, DOODLE, STICK!

3 things i learnt!

1)_____ ☐

2)_____ ☐

3)_____ ☐

One interesting fact about today?

_____
_____
_____
_____
_____

Did you eat anything delicious today?

_____
_____
_____
_____
_____
_____
_____
_____
_____
_____
_____
_____
_____
_____
_____

Where Am I? _____

WEATHER REPORT:

Hot	Mild
Cloudy	Stormy
Raining	windy
Snowing	Sunny
cold	Hail

OTHER?: _____

TODAY I FEEL...

Circle one!

BEST THING ABOUT TODAY?

_____
_____
_____
_____
_____

WHAT I DID TODAY.........DRAW, DOODLE, STICK!

3 things i learnt!

1)_____ ☐

2)_____ ☐

3)_____ ☐

One interesting fact about today?

_____
_____
_____
_____

Anything you can stick in? e.g. tickets!

Where Am I? _____

Date: _____
M T W T F S S

WEATHER REPORT:

Hot   Mild

Cloudy   Stormy

Raining   windy

Snowing   Sunny

cold   Hail

OTHER?: _____

TODAY I FEEL...

Circle one!

BEST THING ABOUT TODAY?

_____
_____
_____
_____
_____
_____

WHAT I DID TODAY..........DRAW, DOODLE, STICK!

3 things i learnt!

1)_____ ☐

2)_____ ☐

3)_____ ☐

One interesting fact about today?

_____
_____
_____
_____

Did You See anything strange or unusual today?

Where Am I? _____

WEATHER REPORT:

Hot	Mild
Cloudy	Stormy
Raining	windy
Snowing	Sunny
cold	Hail

OTHER?: _____

TODAY I FEEL...

Circle one!

BEST THING ABOUT TODAY?

_____
_____
_____
_____
_____

WHAT I DID TODAY..........DRAW, DOODLE, STICK!

3 things i learnt!

1)_____ ☐

2)_____ ☐

3)_____ ☐

One interesting fact about today?

_____
_____
_____
_____
_____

Visit any new places today?

Where Am I? _____

Date: [ ]
M T W T F S S

WEATHER REPORT:

Hot	Mild
Cloudy	Stormy
Raining	windy
Snowing	Sunny
cold	Hail

OTHER?: _____

TODAY I FEEL...

Circle one!

BEST THING ABOUT TODAY?

_____
_____
_____
_____
_____

WHAT I DID TODAY.........DRAW, DOODLE, STICK!

3 things i learnt!

1)_____ [ ]

2)_____ [ ]

3)_____ [ ]

One interesting fact about today?

_____
_____
_____
_____
_____

Pick a great memory - doodle about it?

Where Am I?_____

Date:
M T W T F S S

WEATHER REPORT:

Hot   Mild

Cloudy   Stormy

Raining   windy

Snowing   Sunny

cold   Hail

OTHER?: _____

TODAY I FEEL...

Circle one!

BEST THING ABOUT TODAY?

WHAT I DID TODAY..........DRAW, DOODLE, STICK!

3 things i learnt!

1)_____ ☐

2)_____ ☐

3)_____ ☐

One interesting fact about today?

Your FREE Space! Go craazzy!

Where Am I? _____

Date: _____
M T W T F S S

WEATHER REPORT:

Hot   Mild
Cloudy   Stormy
Raining   windy
Snowing   Sunny
cold   Hail
OTHER?: _____

TODAY I FEEL...

Circle one!

BEST THING ABOUT TODAY?

_____
_____
_____
_____
_____

WHAT I DID TODAY..........DRAW, DOODLE, STICK!

3 things i learnt!

1)_____ ☐

2)_____ ☐

3)_____ ☐

One interesting fact about today?

_____
_____
_____
_____
_____

Did you try anything new today?

Where Am I? _____

Date: _____
M T W T F S S

WEATHER REPORT:

Hot	Mild
Cloudy	Stormy
Raining	windy
Snowing	Sunny
cold	Hail

OTHER?: _____

TODAY I FEEL...

Circle one!

BEST THING ABOUT TODAY?

_____
_____
_____
_____
_____

WHAT I DID TODAY..........DRAW, DOODLE, STICK!

3 things i learnt!

1) _____ ☐

2) _____ ☐

3) _____ ☐

One interesting fact about today?

_____
_____
_____
_____

Did you eat anything delicious today?

Made in the USA
Middletown, DE
20 June 2022

67432677R00064